Nelson Spelling

Spelling 5

Denis and Helen Ballance

Thomas Nelson & Sons Limited
Lincoln Way, Windmill Road,
Sunbury-on-Thames, Middlesex TW16 7HP
P.O. Box 73146 Nairobi Kenya
P.O. Box 943 95 Church Street Kingston Jamaica
308–312 Lockhart Road Golden Coronation Building
2nd Floor Blk. A Hong Kong
29 Jalan Bangau Singapore 28

Thomas Nelson (Australia) Limited
19–39 Jeffcott Street West Melbourne Victoria 3003

Thomas Nelson & Sons (Canada) Limited
81 Curlew Drive Don Mills Ontario

Thomas Nelson (Nigeria) Limited
8 Ilupeju Bypass PMB 21303 Ikeja Lagos

© Denis and Helen Ballance 1979
Illustrated by Bucken Ltd., Alan Ward & Peter Joyce
Designed by John A. Willis
© Illustrations by Thomas Nelson & Sons Limited
First published 1979

ISBN   0 17 424235 2

Printed in Hong Kong

Nelson Spelling

Book 5

The best way to improve your spelling is to learn a few new words every day. The 800 words in this book have been chosen because they are the ones you are most likely to need at this stage of your school life. Each page provides one week's work. There are five words to be learnt on each of the first four days of the week. For Fridays, there are some puzzles for you to do. The puzzles are designed to help you to look at the shapes of words, to study the order in which the letters come and to practise using the words in sentences. You may have a weekly spelling test based on the words in the lists as well.

There are no spelling rules in this book. Most of the rules do not work very well and they are all hard to understand.

The 'Just for Fun' pages may be done at any time. On the back cover there is a group of words which most people find difficult to learn.

For some of the puzzles, you will find a supply of squared paper useful. Please do not write the answers to the puzzles in this book.

For the Teacher

The word list for this book is printed in alphabetical order on page 48 and inside the back cover. It contains the words which the authors consider children of this age use most frequently. Special attention has been paid to subject vocabularies and selected proper names are also included. Some words which present particular difficulty are repeated from earlier books in this series.

Grading of difficulty within each book was held to be of less significance than the overall grading of the series. Nevertheless, there is a background gradation within each book although this has been set aside where words on a particular theme are grouped together.

The authors have avoided grouping words of similar structure pattern together since it is held that a group such as 'hand, band, sand, land, wand' encourages superficial learning. Such grouping discourages one of the basic objectives of the series—the careful examination of the structure of each word.

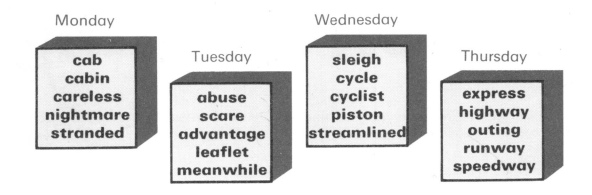

Monday
cab
cabin
careless
nightmare
stranded

Tuesday
abuse
scare
advantage
leaflet
meanwhile

Wednesday
sleigh
cycle
cyclist
piston
streamlined

Thursday
express
highway
outing
runway
speedway

1 Add a word from the second box to one from the first to make a list word.

high	stream
leaf	night
mean	care
cab	speed

mare	less
way	while
lined	in
let	way

2 Change two letters in each of these words to make a list word.

listen   scalp
impress   basin
strained   mouse
clueless   eating

3 Write list words which mean:

a) slipshod, not taking care.
b) a very unpleasant dream.
c) very fast.   d) main road.
e) to frighten.   f) to insult.
g) a taxi.   h) part of an engine.
i) motorcycle racing sport.
j) abandoned, left high and dry.
k) an excursion or trip.
l) land strip for aircraft.

4 Solve these puzzles to make list words.

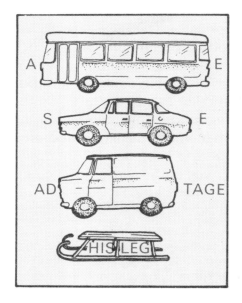

A ___ E

S ___ E

AD ___ TAGE

HIS LEG

four

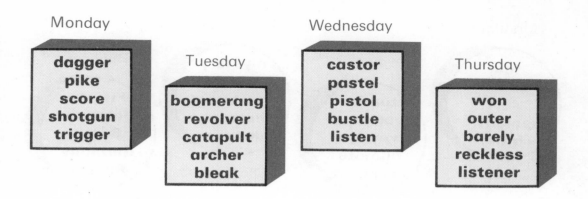

Monday
dagger
pike
score
shotgun
trigger

Tuesday
boomerang
revolver
catapult
archer
bleak

Wednesday
castor
pastel
pistol
bustle
listen

Thursday
won
outer
barely
reckless
listener

1 *Write these sentences. Fill each space with a word from the lists.*
a) The _____ shot an arrow which _____ missed the bull's eye.
b) Then he fired a _____ shot which landed in the _____ ring of the target.
c) His final _____ was fifteen less than that of the man who _____.

2 *Copy this frame. Write the words from Wednesday's list into it in alphabetical order.*

		S	T		
		S	T		
		S	T		
		S	T		
		S	T		

→

3 *Change the order of the letters in these shapes to make their names.*

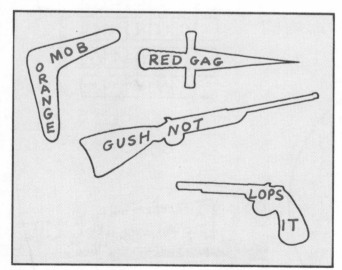

4 *Write a list word which means:*
a) small wheel fixed to a chair leg. *b)* cheerless.
c) someone who listens.
d) rash. *e)* finger piece for firing a gun.
f) opposite of inner.

5 *Change one letter in each of these words to make a list word.*
son   scone   piston   like   danger   break   otter   rarely

five

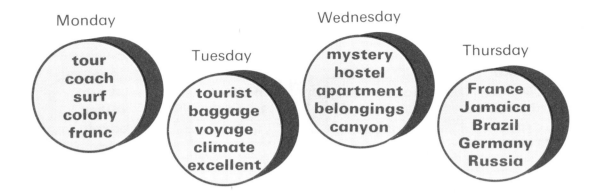

Monday

tour
coach
surf
colony
franc

Tuesday

tourist
baggage
voyage
climate
excellent

Wednesday

mystery
hostel
apartment
belongings
canyon

Thursday

France
Jamaica
Brazil
Germany
Russia

1 *Write these sentences. Use words from the lists to fill the spaces.*

a) On the first night of our _____ of Germany, the _____ stopped at Aachen.
b) Jamaica has _____ sandy beaches which are ideal for _____ boarding.
c) The _____ of northern Russia is too cold for the average _____.

2 *Add the missing letters to make list words.*

	L	O	N	G			
		M	A	N		
P	A	R	T			
		M	A	T		
	C	E	L	L		
	O	U	R			
		G	A	G		
A	N	Y		

3 *Copy this puzzle. Fill in the missing letters to make the names of the countries in Thursday's list.*

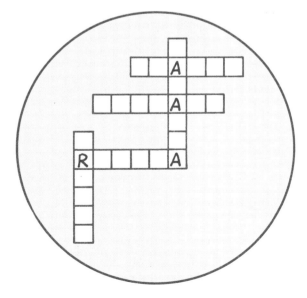

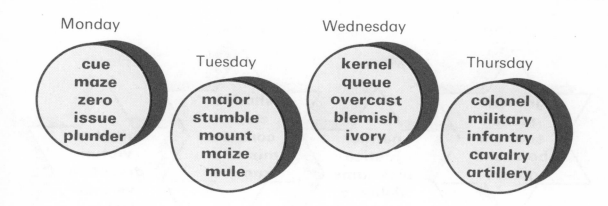

Monday

cue
maze
zero
issue
plunder

Tuesday

major
stumble
mount
maize
mule

Wednesday

kernel
queue
overcast
blemish
ivory

Thursday

colonel
military
infantry
cavalry
artillery

1 Write list words which mean:

a) to give out. b) cloudy.
c) cross between horse and donkey.
d) to miss one's footing.
e) spot or stain. f) nothing.
g) loot, booty, something stolen.

2 Write list words ending in **-ry** which mean:

a) elephant tusk. b) foot soldiers. c) mobile guns.
d) mounted soldiers.
e) having to do with the army.

3 Draw each picture and choose a word from the box to go with it.

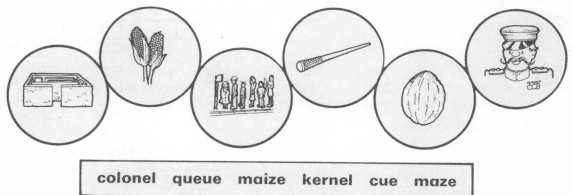

| colonel | queue | maize | kernel | cue | maze |

4 Complete this limerick with words from Tuesday's list.

There was an old _____ named Poole.
Who went for a ride on a _____.
His unusual _____.
Put him out for the count,
And made poor old Poole look a fool.

5 Find the five list words hidden in this letter line.

MAZEROVERCASTUMBLEMISH

Can you find five other words?

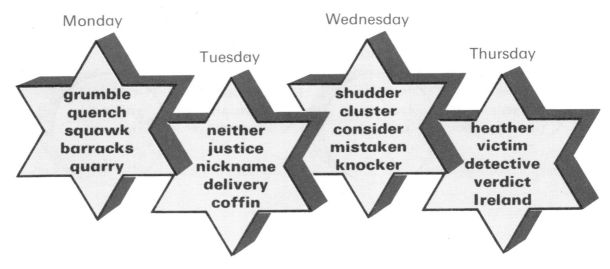

Monday
grumble
quench
squawk
barracks
quarry

Tuesday
neither
justice
nickname
delivery
coffin

Wednesday
shudder
cluster
consider
mistaken
knocker

Thursday
heather
victim
detective
verdict
Ireland

1 *Write these sentences. Use words from the lists to fill the spaces.*

a) The _____ was knocked down by a _____ van while he was chasing a criminal.

b) At the Coroner's Court, the _____ was that the _____ died from natural causes.

c) _____ the man's friends nor his relations thought that _____ had been done.

2 *Fill in the missing letters to make list words.*

	R	U	M		
		S	T	A	K	E	
			T	H	E	
		L	I	V	E	
			O	F	F	
			S	I	D	E	

3 *Copy this puzzle on to squared paper. Fill in the missing letters to make list words.* The green *panel will spell a girl's name.*

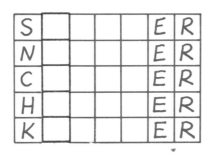

S				E	R
N				E	R
C				E	R
H				E	R
K				E	R

4 *Put these short words together so as to make five list words.*

BAR
ICE   LAND   AT
NAME   RACKS
JUST
HE   NICK   HER
IRE

eight

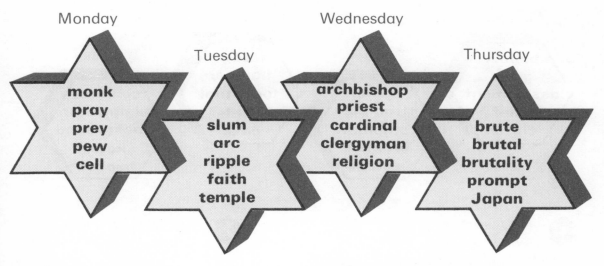

Monday: monk, pray, prey, pew, cell

Tuesday: slum, arc, ripple, faith, temple

Wednesday: archbishop, priest, cardinal, clergyman, religion

Thursday: brute, brutal, brutality, prompt, Japan

1 *Write list words which mean:*
a) a priest who lives in a monastery.
b) a small wave.   *c)* part of a circle.
d) A very senior priest in the Roman
Catholic Church who helps to choose a
new Pope.   *e)* a creature which is
hunted for food.   *f)* country in eastern
Asia.   *g)* the cruel use of force.
h) a poor district of a town.

2 *Write these sentences. Choose the correct spellings to complete them.*
a) The priest kneels before
the altar to (prey/pray).
b) Each monk lives in a
bare, cold (cell/sell).
c) God told Noah to build
an (arc/ark).

3 *Copy this puzzle on to squared paper. Write in list words to complete it.*
The green panel spells the shape's name.

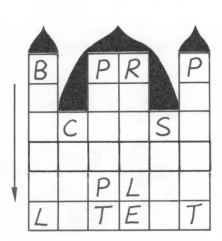

4 *Change the first two letters in each of the following to make a list word.*

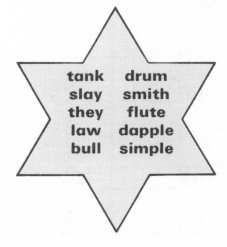

tank   drum
slay   smith
they   flute
law   dapple
bull   simple

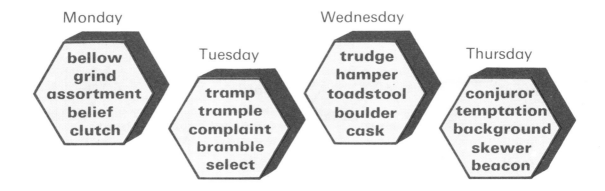

Monday
bellow grind assortment belief clutch

Tuesday
tramp trample complaint bramble select

Wednesday
trudge hamper toadstool boulder cask

Thursday
conjuror temptation background skewer beacon

1 *Find words in the lists which mean:*

a) to tread under foot. b) to grasp.
c) a large wicker basket. d) mixture.
e) to walk slowly and heavily.
f) to roar like a bull. g) to choose.
h) a warning light. i) a large rock.
j) metal spike for securing meat.
k) to reduce to small pieces.
l) blackberry bush.

2 *Rearrange the letters in these shapes to make their names.*

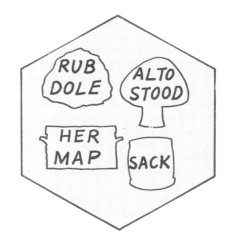

3 *Use list words to complete this puzzle.*

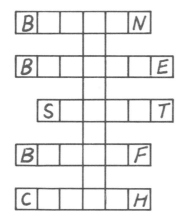

4 *Make these into list words by adding one letter.*

tram ramble elect ask below bacon rind bolder sewer

ten

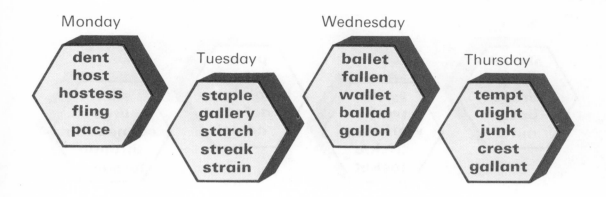

Monday
dent
host
hostess
fling
pace

Tuesday
staple
gallery
starch
streak
strain

Wednesday
ballet
fallen
wallet
ballad
gallon

Thursday
tempt
alight
junk
crest
gallant

1 Write these sentences. Fill each space with a word from the lists.

a) If you leave your _____ sticking out of your pocket, it may _____ someone to steal it.

b) Mr Reed said that a lamp post had _____ on his car and made a _____ in the roof.

c) He sang the _____ so quietly that people sitting in the _____ could not hear the words.

2 Copy this frame. Write words from Tuesday's list into it so that the green panel spells the name of a fruit.

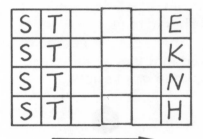

S	T			E
S	T			K
S	T			N
S	T			H

→

3 Take two letters from each of these words to make a list word.

junket
honest
decent
packet
tempest
filling

4 Write the list word which can have either of these meanings.

a) to step down from a bus/on fire

b) top of a wave/badge or emblem

c) Chinese ship/rubbish or garbage

5 Put **all** into each of these sets of letters to make a list word.
Example: **gant → gallant**

        bet   wet   gery   fen   bad   gon

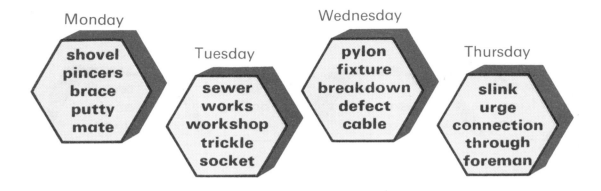

Monday
**shovel
pincers
brace
putty
mate**

Tuesday
**sewer
works
workshop
trickle
socket**

Wednesday
**pylon
fixture
breakdown
defect
cable**

Thursday
**slink
urge
connection
through
foreman**

1 *Write these sentences. Use words from the lists to fill the spaces.*

a) There has been a_____ in the electricity supply this morning because of a _____ in an underground _____.

b) A _____ of water from a cracked _____ pipe leaked _____ the cable's covering and caused a short circuit.

c) The _____ in charge of the repair gang said that they would try to make a _____ as soon as possible.

2 *Take letters from the end of the first name and the beginning of the second to make list words.*

Example: **Arth(ur Ge)nt → urge
Patrick Leedham
Monica Blenkinsop
Denise Werner
Douglas Linklater
Thelma Teesdale**

3 *Write list words to fit these pictures and meanings.*

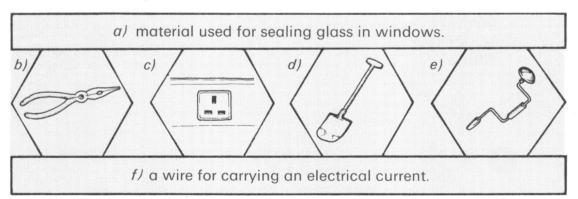

a) material used for sealing glass in windows.

b)

c)

d)

e)

f) a wire for carrying an electrical current.

JUST FOR FUN

 1 *Solve this crossword by making anagrams of the clues. 1 down is done for you.*

	1 A		2		3
4 S					
I					
5 D					
E					

Across: 4 MASTER   5 LEADER
Down: 1 IDEAS   2 ORGAN   3 SPEAR

2 *Find the names of the parts of a car hidden in these pairs of words.*
Example: **w(heat er)ect → heater**

fuse atoms
empty reel
new heels
clasp rings
taboo topic
harpist only
zebra keeper
ribbon network
most arteries
rich ornament

 3

 The Rev. W. Spooner was famous for mixing up the beginnings of words. He would say things like **tough and rumble** when he meant **rough and tumble.** Expressions like these are called **spoonerisms**

 This girl also mixes up the beginnings of words. Her name is Molly Jones, but she calls herself Jolly Mones. Here are some of her sayings. *What do you think she meant to say? Can you make up some spoonerisms of your own?*

a) It's a wrong load that has no turning.   b) The fled rag is flying.
c) Riding along on the west of the crave.   d) Open a bin of teans.
e) The police should damp clown on crime.   f) a day's ready stain.

 4 *Write words that begin and end with the same letter to fit these meanings.*
a) a slice of bacon.   b) not low.   c) to hit a door with a clenched fist.
d) a ray of moonlight.   e) to get well after an illness.   f) midday.

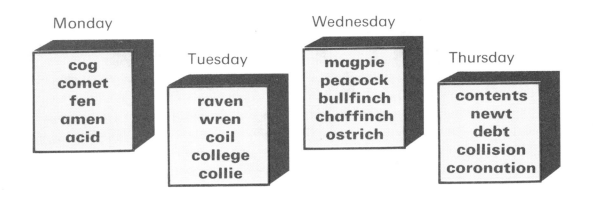

Monday: cog comet fen amen acid

Tuesday: raven wren coil college collie

Wednesday: magpie peacock bullfinch chaffinch ostrich

Thursday: contents newt debt collision coronation

1 *Copy this frame. Complete it with list words which fit the clues.*

C	O		toothed wheel
C	O			spiral
C	O				travelling star
C	O					sheepdog
C	O						school for older pupils
C	O							what is contained
C	O								crash
C	O									royal crowning

2 *Rearrange the letters in these shapes to make bird names from the Wednesday list.*

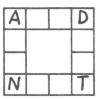

FILL BUNCH

CHIN CHAFF

COP CAKE

AIM PEG

3 *Find the list words contained within these longer words.*

**lamentation indefensible
Lawrence recognition**

4 *Copy this puzzle. Complete it with words from the lists.*

A		D
N		T

5 *Take two letters from each of the following to make a list word.*

comment rancid often newest warren stamen

fourteen

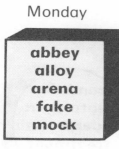

Monday

abbey
alloy
arena
fake
mock

Tuesday

barter
banner
bisect
murmur
ramble

Wednesday

sprawl
thoughtful
Wales
Scotland
stubborn

Thursday

autumn
conclude
burrow
resign
headline

1 Copy these frames on to squared paper. Write words from the lists into them. If your answers are correct the numbers in the green panels will add up to eleven.

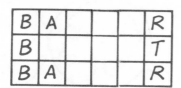

2 Copy this limerick. Fill the spaces with words from Wednesday's list.

A _____ old lady from _____
Had a _____ attachment to snails.
She allowed them to _____
All over the hall,
And never put salt on their tails.

3 Find list words which mean:
a) to bring to an end.
b) a mixture of metals.
c) to divide into two equal parts.
d) a low sound.
e) the exchange of goods for other goods.
f) not genuine.
g) the season when leaves fall.

4 Make a list word by changing the first letter of these words.
gamble bake lock manner
furrow sales carter design

fifteen

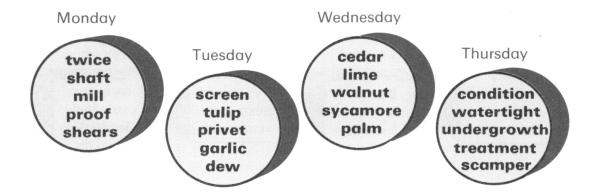

Monday: twice, shaft, mill, proof, shears

Tuesday: screen, tulip, privet, garlic, dew

Wednesday: cedar, lime, walnut, sycamore, palm

Thursday: condition, watertight, undergrowth, treatment, scamper

1 *Write these sentences. Use words from the lists to fill the spaces.*

a) A thick privet hedge makes a good _____ but you must cut it with sharp _____ at least _____ a year.

b) The _____ bulbs have been given special _____ to ensure that they reach you in good _____.

c) We needed _____ boots in the mornings because the dense _____ was drenched with _____.

2 *Rearrange the letters in these shapes to make names of trees.*

RACED

NUT LAW

MILE

MAY SCORE

3 *Take letters from the end of the first word and from the beginning of the second to make list words.*
Example: **ro(de w)ell → dew**

twice darned
slim excuse
opal magnate
deprive temporarily
Spanish afternoon
sugar licking

4 *Add one letter to the beginning of each word to make a list word.*

rivet
hears
roof
camper
ill
haft

sixteen

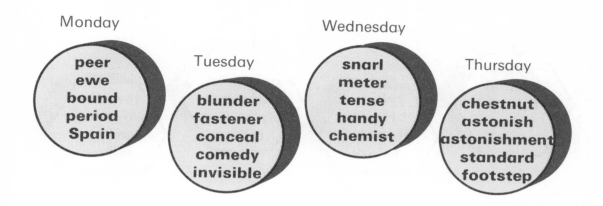

Monday
peer
ewe
bound
period
Spain

Tuesday
blunder
fastener
conceal
comedy
invisible

Wednesday
snarl
meter
tense
handy
chemist

Thursday
chestnut
astonish
astonishment
standard
footstep

1 *Write list words which mean:*

a) a female sheep. *b)* great surprise.
c) hide. *d)* amusing play or film.
e) a mistake. *f)* an angry sound.
g) to look closely. *h)* a springing leap.
i) not seen. *j)* useful, ready to hand.

2 *Choose the right word.*

pier/peer   yew/ewe

meter/metre

3 *Copy these frames on squared paper. Fill in the missing letters to make list words.*

a)   *b)*

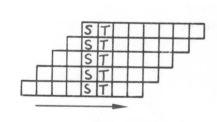

4 *Add two letters to each of these words to make a list word.*

ten   come   met   under   bud   prod   pin   visible   and

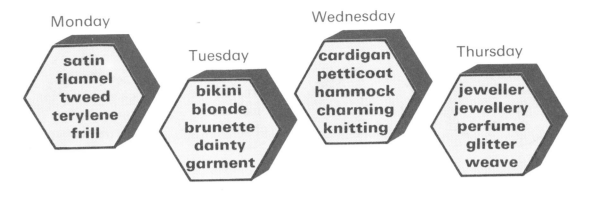

Monday
satin
flannel
tweed
terylene
frill

Tuesday
bikini
blonde
brunette
dainty
garment

Wednesday
cardigan
petticoat
hammock
charming
knitting

Thursday
jeweller
jewellery
perfume
glitter
weave

1 *Write list words which mean:*
a) having light-coloured hair.   b) scent.
c) to make cloth on a loom.   d) garment worn under a dress.   e) a scanty swimsuit.
f) hand process for making garments by the use of long needles.   g) a portable bed.
h) man-made fibre.   i) a thin band of pleated material used for trimming.
j) collective name for rings, brooches, etc.

2 *Put these short words together to make four list words.*

car	tic
sat	ham
dig	in
mock	an
oat	pet

3 *Make list words by:*
a) *adding one letter*
**weed   harming   fill
litter   kitting   wave**

b) *changing two letters*
**baton   channel   cardinal
shinty   haddock   hiking**

4 *Use list words to name:*
a) one shopkeeper.
b) two hair colours.
c) three garments.
d) four fabrics.

knitting hammock

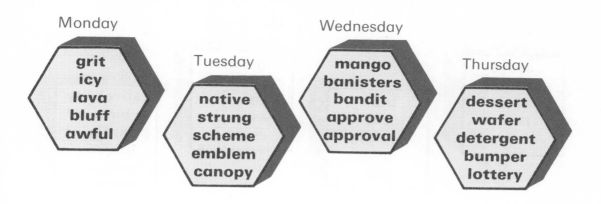

Monday: **grit icy lava bluff awful**

Tuesday: **native strung scheme emblem canopy**

Wednesday: **mango banisters bandit approve approval**

Thursday: **dessert wafer detergent bumper lottery**

1 Copy this frame. Write list words into it to fit the clues.

a) the sweet course of a meal. →
b) a raffle or game of chance. →
c) liquid for dissolving grease. →
d) a thin biscuit for ice cream. →
e) guard rail on a car or lorry. →

D			E	R			
L			E	R			
			E	R			
			E	R			
B			E	R			

The green panel.

2 Take letters from the end of the first word and from the beginning of the second to make list words.

Cuban ditty
Lapp rover
Slav agent

Viking rites
German goblet
Celtic youth

3 Copy this puzzle. Use list words to complete it.

4 Fit each pair of letters into the word alongside them to make a list word.

an copy　**fu awl**　**fe war**
nd bait　**tr sung**　**ti nave**

5 Find list words which mean:
a) guard rail on a staircase.　b) tropical fruit.　c) molten rock.
d) awning or cover.　e) badge.

nineteen

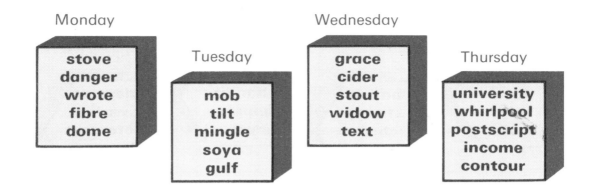

Monday

stove
danger
wrote
fibre
dome

Tuesday

mob
tilt
mingle
soya
gulf

Wednesday

grace
cider
stout
widow
text

Thursday

university
whirlpool
postscript
income
contour

1 *Write list words which mean:*

a) money coming in.   b) something added to a letter.   c) a place of higher education.
d) a line on a map joining places of equal height.   e) a woman whose husband has died.
f) a bean which is rich in protein.   g) fat.
h) water swirling in a circle.   i) a drink made from fermented apple juice.
j) a hemispherical structure on top of a building.   k) to lean to one side.
l) a deep inlet of the sea.

2 *Take letters from the end of the first word and the beginning of the second to make list words.*

calm observation
thrilling race
decide rightly
best overalls
until tomorrow
merest outline

3 *Rearrange the letters in these words to make words from Monday's list.*

garden   mode   votes
brief   tower

4 *Change one letter to make a list word.*

write   scout   shove
brace   kilt   single

5 *Find three words in the lists which begin and end with the same letter.*

twenty

1 Change the order of the letters in these shapes to make the names of birds.

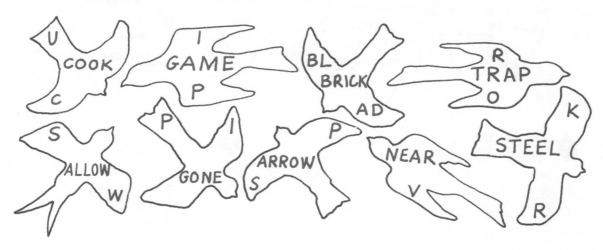

COOK U C

GAME I P

BL BRICK AD

R TRAP O

S ALLOW W

P GONE I S

P ARROW

NEAR V

K STEEL R

2 This word chain is made by adding one letter at a time.
i → in → fin → fine → fines → finest   Each link is a real word.
Write and complete these word chains.

a) **a** → _____ → _____ → **rang** → _____ → **orange**
b) **a** → _____ → _____ → **late** → _____ → **slater**
c) **a** → _____ → _____ → **rate** → _____ → **grater**
d) **a** → _____ → _____ → **heat** → _____ → **sheath**
e) **on** → _____ → _____ → **hones** → _____ → **honesty**

3 Can you write what Jolly Mones meant when she said:

a) Will you lend me your pelt fen?
b) I saw some leep and shambs.
c) It was raining dats and cogs.
d) Have you loaded the wish dasher?
e) The judge said that the cashier
was trying to book the cooks.

4 Add three letters to the words in the shapes to make the names of tools.

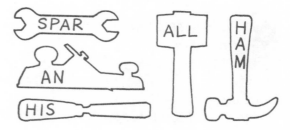

SPAR

ALL

HA M

AN

HIS

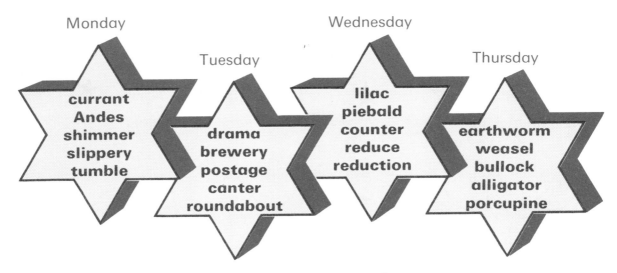

Monday: currant, Andes, shimmer, slippery, tumble

Tuesday: drama, brewery, postage, canter, roundabout

Wednesday: lilac, piebald, counter, reduce, reduction

Thursday: earthworm, weasel, bullock, alligator, porcupine

 1 *Write these sentences. Use words from the lists to fill the spaces.*

a) If you hand in the parcel at the post office _____, they will tell you how much the _____ will cost.

b) When approaching a _____, you should _____ speed and give way to traffic coming from the right.

2 *Copy this puzzle. Fill in the missing letters to make list words.*

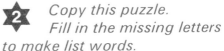
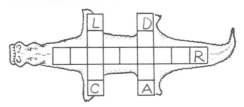

 3 *Rearrange the letters in these shapes to make words from the lists.*

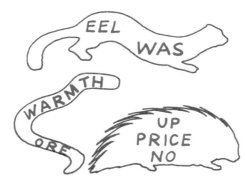

 4 *Add letters to make list words.*

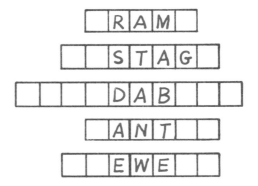

 5 *Write list words meaning:*

a) a colour of horses.   b) a large reptile.

c) a flower.   d) a mountain range.   e) dried grape.   f) soil-boring creature.

Put their first letters together to make a royal house.

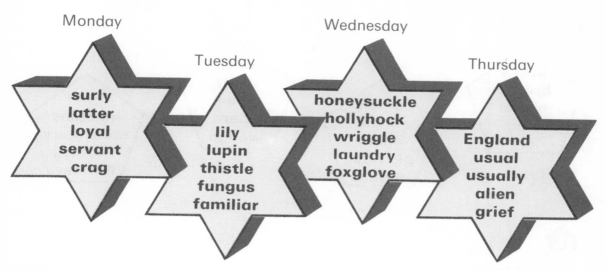

Monday: surly, latter, loyal, servant, crag

Tuesday: lily, lupin, thistle, fungus, familiar

Wednesday: honeysuckle, hollyhock, wriggle, laundry, foxglove

Thursday: England, usual, usually, alien, grief

 1 *Write list words which are opposite in meaning to:*

a) cheerful, good-tempered.
b) master.   c) treacherous.
d) former.   e) native born.
f) not well-known.   g) seldom.
h) great happiness.

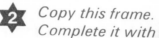 **2** *Copy this frame. Complete it with list words. The green panel spells out the name of the shape.*

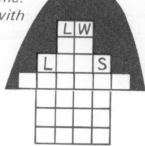

 3 *Rearrange the letters in each of these flowers to make its name.*

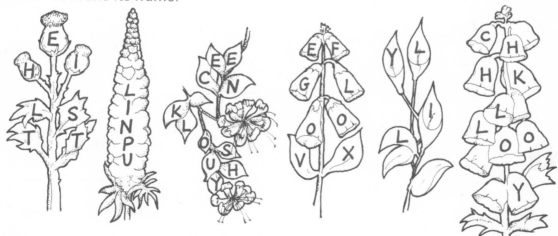

 4 *Make six list words from the letters in this line.*

CRAGRIEFUNGUSUALIENGLAND

Can you find six other words?

 5 *Change one letter in each of these to make a list word.*

drag   litter   brief
lilt   royal   curly

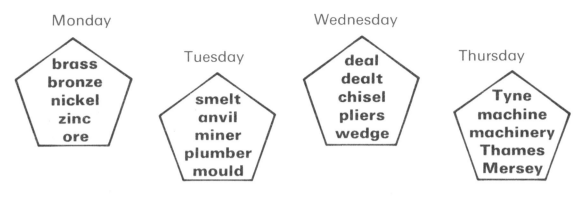

Monday: brass bronze nickel zinc ore

Tuesday: smelt anvil miner plumber mould

Wednesday: deal dealt chisel pliers wedge

Thursday: Tyne machine machinery Thames Mersey

1 Fill in the missing letters to make list words which are:

a) names of metals.	b) names of things made of metal.
▢ I N ▢ ▢ O N ▢ ▢ A S ▢	▢ H I S ▢ ▢ ▢ L I E ▢ ▢ ▢ C H I N ▢

2 Use list words to name these pictures.

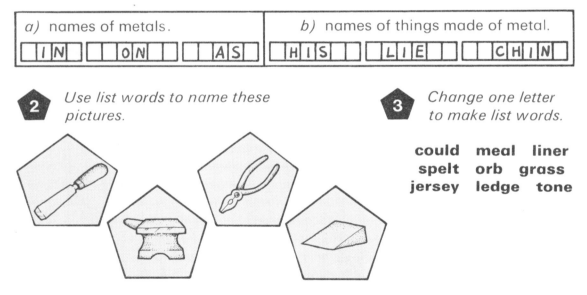

3 Change one letter to make list words.

could   meal   liner
spelt   orb   grass
jersey   ledge   tone

4 Write this limerick.
Fill the spaces with list words.

There once was a _____ named Green
Who invented a splendid _____.
It used _____ and _____
And lots of red ink
To _____ statuettes of the Queen.

5 Take letters from the end of the first word and from the beginning of the second to make list words.
Example: **snowball(s melt)ing**

Norman village   raw edged
carmine robes   ideal terms
made allies   minor errors

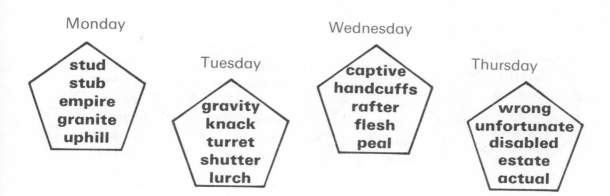

Monday

stud
stub
empire
granite
uphill

Tuesday

gravity
knack
turret
shutter
lurch

Wednesday

captive
handcuffs
rafter
flesh
peal

Thursday

wrong
unfortunate
disabled
estate
actual

1 Write these sentences. Use words from the lists to fill the spaces.

a) The _____ was locked up in the highest _____ of the castle.

b) He was fastened by chains and _____ to the cold _____ wall.

c) A heavy _____ covered the only window and the _____ prisoner lived in total darkness.

2 Find list words which begin and end with the same letter to fit these meanings.

a) wooden roof support.
b) crippled, lacking mobility.
c) a special skill or trick.
d) country ruled by an emperor.
e) tower rising above a castle
f) a large holding of land.

3 Copy this frame on to squared paper. Complete it with words from Monday's and Tuesday's lists.

The green panel names the shape.

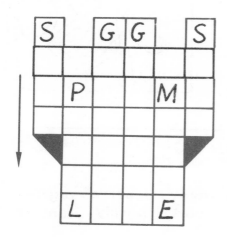

4 Rearrange the letters in these anagrams to make list words.

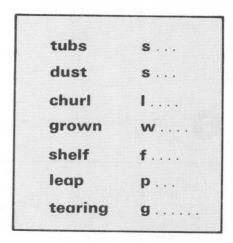

tubs	s . . .
dust	s . . .
churl	l . . . .
grown	w . . . .
shelf	f . . . .
leap	p . . .
tearing	g . . . . . .

Monday
bison
moose
tiger
tigress
remote

Tuesday
whip
defy
worry
anxiety
rarely

Wednesday
replace
authority
hurl
resemble
sweat

Thursday
reject
remnant
reserve
convey
curse

1 *Write these sentences. Choose words from Tuesday's and Wednesday's lists to fill the spaces.*

The regular animal trainer was ill and the man who was chosen to _____ him _____ had anything to do with the big cats. As soon as they came into the ring, the tigers sensed the trainer's _____ and began to _____ him. The new trainer tried to assert his _____ by cracking the _____. The tigress seized the whip and began to _____ it while her mate chose that moment to _____ himself upon the trainer's back.

2 *Copy these two puzzles. Complete them by writing in words from the lists.*

R	E			R		
R	E			A		
R	E			M		

R	E			C		
R	E			A	
R	E			T	

3 *Make list words by:*

a) adding one letter.	*b) changing one letter.*
hip eject cure seat covey tier	mouse deny deserve digress sorry curl barely remove

Monday
stump
style
turf
blossom
bridle

Tuesday
referee
penalty
versus
league
qualify

Wednesday
umpire
wicket
boundary
applaud
applause

Thursday
billiards
autograph
championship
wrestling
hockey

1 *Write these sentences. Use words from the lists to fill the spaces.*

a) In cricket, one _____ stands behind the _____ at the end opposite to the batsman.

b) The opening batsman was given a round of _____ when he hit a six over the _____.

c) Both soccer and _____ are played on _____ pitches.

3 *Find a list word which means:*

a) cheers and clapping.

b) signature of a well-known person.

c) the limits of a cricket pitch.

d) game played with a cue.

2 *Make list words by:*
a) adding two letters.

refer
bloom
resting
ague
sty
ride

b) changing two letters.

monkey
racket
burn
clump
applied
expire

4 *Which list word does v. stand for?*

MANCHESTER CITY v. ARSENAL

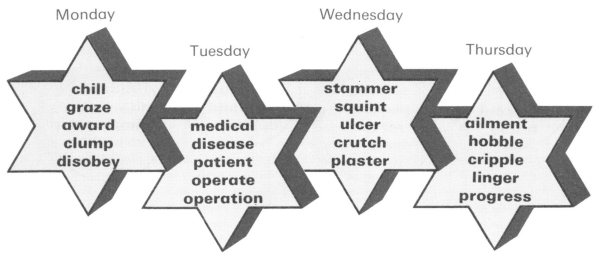

Monday: chill, graze, award, clump, disobey

Tuesday: medical, disease, patient, operate, operation

Wednesday: stammer, squint, ulcer, crutch, plaster

Thursday: ailment, hobble, cripple, linger, progress

1 *Write these sentences. Use words from the lists to fill the spaces.*

a) The _____ with the broken leg has had it put in _____.

b) He should be able to _____ along the ward with the aid of a _____.

c) This boy will need an _____ on his eye to cure the _____.

2 *Add two letters to the beginning and two to the end of each of these to make a list word.*

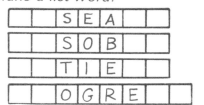

		S	E	A		
		S	O	B		
		T	I	E		
		O	G	R	E	

3 *Rearrange these letters to make list words connected with illness and medicine. The first letter of each answer is given.*

cruel → u   stapler → p

seaside → d   tea pint → p

met rams → s   poet era → o

in metal → a   dim lace → m

4 *Add one letter to each of these words to make a list word.*

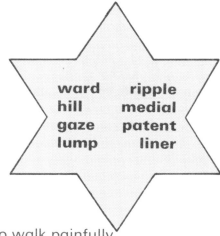

ward   ripple
hill   medial
gaze   patent
lump   liner

5 *Write list words which mean:*

a) an eye defect.   b) a speech defect.   c) to walk painfully.

d) something given for merit.   e) to make a small wound in the skin.

twenty-eight

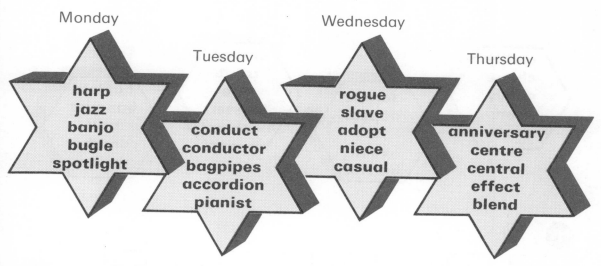

Monday
**harp
jazz
banjo
bugle
spotlight**

Tuesday
**conduct
conductor
bagpipes
accordion
pianist**

Wednesday
**rogue
slave
adopt
niece
casual**

Thursday
**anniversary
centre
central
effect
blend**

1 *Write these sentences. Use words from the lists to fill the spaces.*

a) The _____ sat with his hands poised above the keyboard waiting for the _____ to begin the concerto.

b) A piper marched up and down the castle ramparts playing the _____ on the _____ of the battle.

c) The lead guitarist stood under a _____ in the _____ of the stage.

2 *Replace each* **x** *with a consonant to make names of musical instruments from the lists.*

a) **xuxx**e
b) **xaxxixex**
c) a**xxoxxiox**
d) **xaxx**
e) **xax xo**

3 *Take letters from the end of the first word and from the beginning of the second to make list words.*
Example: **he(ro gue)sses**

adjacent regions   **urban jollity**
press lavender   **recent rally**
Olympian isthmus   **broad option**
Brownie ceremony   **silicon ducts**

4 *Find list words which mean:*

a) the middle point.
b) sister's or brother's daughter.
c) informal, free and easy.
d) person of bad reputation.
e) to mix in together.
f) to take something over.
g) to bring something about.

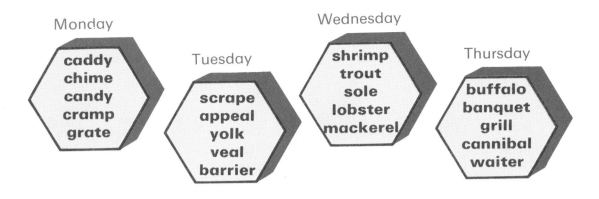

Monday: caddy, chime, candy, cramp, grate

Tuesday: scrape, appeal, yolk, veal, barrier

Wednesday: shrimp, trout, sole, lobster, mackerel

Thursday: buffalo, banquet, grill, cannibal, waiter

1 *Add the missing letters to make words from the lists.*

| | P | E | A | |
| | R | A | T | |

| | H | I | M | |
| | | R | A | P |

| | R | A | M | |
| | A | D | D | |

| | A | N | D | |
| | | R | I | M |

2 *Write this limerick. Fill the spaces with words from Thursday's list.*

There was a young man named Hannibal
Who went out to dine with a ———.
The main course, a mixed ———,
Contained ——— Bill,
A ———, two cooks and poor Hannibal.

3 *Rearrange the letters in these shapes to make their names.*

CRAM KEEL
BOLSTER
LOSE
OR TUT

4 *Change the first and last letters of these words to make them into list words.*

bold · group · drama
carried
hear · fold · wrath

5 *Find list words which mean:*

a) a container for tea.   b) a feast.   c) the orange part of an egg.
d) the meat of a calf.   e) an obstacle.   f) a fireplace.

thirty

JUST FOR FUN

1 Copy these two puzzles. Complete them with the names of kings and queens of England (EN) or Scotland (SC).

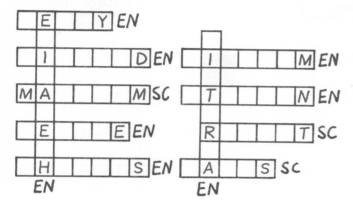

2 Take letters from the end of the first word and the beginning of the second to make names of things you find in a bedroom.

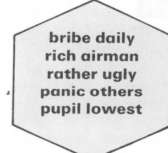

bribe daily
rich airman
rather ugly
panic others
pupil lowest

3  What did Jolly Mones mean when she said?

4 Rearrange the letters inside these symbols to make the names of countries.

a) My favourite meat is boast reef.
b) I think he's getting into weep dater.
c) The motorway was closed by focal log.
d) I was eating a juicy pipe reach.
e) Before you get married you have to but up the panns.
f) Wot heather makes me feel very tired.
g) I don't think he can see the trood for the wees.

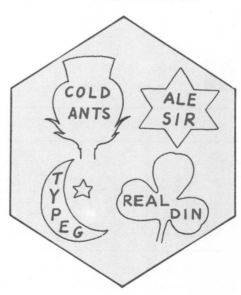

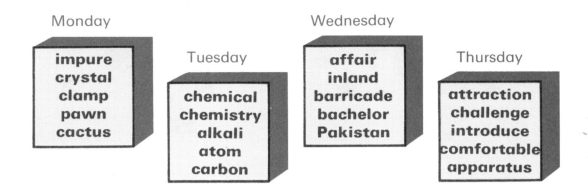

Monday
**impure
crystal
clamp
pawn
cactus**

Tuesday
**chemical
chemistry
alkali
atom
carbon**

Wednesday
**affair
inland
barricade
bachelor
Pakistan**

Thursday
**attraction
challenge
introduce
comfortable
apparatus**

1 *Write these sentences. Use words from the lists to fill the spaces.*

a) Much of the _____ used in _____, such as test tubes and retorts, is made of glass.

b) When air is breathed out of the lungs, it is _____ because it contains too much _____ dioxide.

c) If a soil is too acid, its _____ balance may be improved by adding an _____.

2 *Fill in the missing letters to make list words.*

		F	O	R	T			
		A	C	T				
	T	R	O	D				
	A	C	H	E				
	A	L	L					
		M	I	S	T			
	T	R	A	C	T			

3 *Choose list words to match these pictures and meanings.*

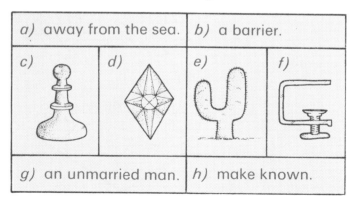

a) away from the sea.	*b)* a barrier.		
c)	*d)*	*e)*	*f)*
g) an unmarried man.	*h)* make known.		

4 *Copy this frame. Complete it with list words.*

I ____ E
A ____ I
C ____ L
A ____ R

thirty-two

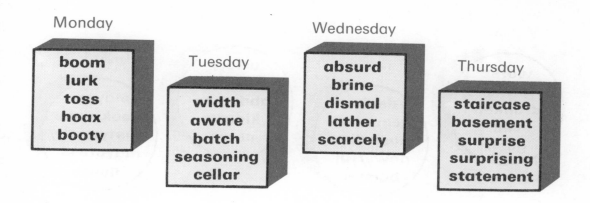

Monday
boom
lurk
toss
hoax
booty

Tuesday
width
aware
batch
seasoning
cellar

Wednesday
absurd
brine
dismal
lather
scarcely

Thursday
staircase
basement
surprise
surprising
statement

1 Write list words which mean:
a) soapy foam. b) salty water.
c) something unexpected.
d) mischievous trick or joke.
e) to throw in the air. f) dreary.
g) an announcement. h) loud noise.
i) ridiculous. j) food flavouring. .
k) group or set. l) stolen goods.

2 Copy this puzzle. Use list words to complete it. The green panel spells the shape's name.

3 Rearrange these sets of letters to make list words showing what is on the other side of each door.

raise
cast

caller

bent
seam

4 Add two letters to each of the following to make a list word.

war   wit   dial   bin
boy   late   to   bat

5 Change one letter to make a list word.

collar   book   lark   gather

thirty-three

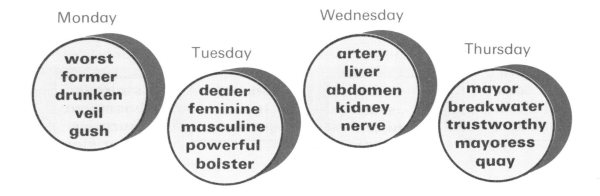

Monday
worst
former
drunken
veil
gush

Tuesday
dealer
feminine
masculine
powerful
bolster

Wednesday
artery
liver
abdomen
kidney
nerve

Thursday
mayor
breakwater
trustworthy
mayoress
quay

1 All the letters in the word **bolster** can be used to make two smaller words.

bolster → lest

bolster → rob

Find the second word to complete these pairs. Use all the letters.

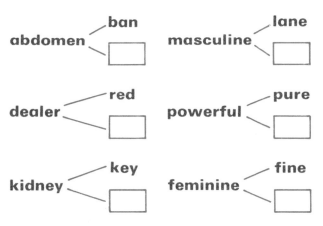

abdomen → ban / [ ]

masculine → lane / [ ]

dealer → red / [ ]

powerful → pure / [ ]

kidney → key / [ ]

feminine → fine / [ ]

3 *Write these sentences. Use words from the lists to fill the spaces.*

a) The heart is a _____ pump which sends blood gushing into every _____ in the body.

b) If mayor is the _____, then _____ must be the feminine.

c) The _____ where ships load and unload is protected from the open sea by a stone _____.

2 *Choose the correct spelling.*

mare
mayor

veil
vale

quay
key

4 *Find list words which mean the opposite of:*

latter
trickle
unreliable
sober
weak
best

thirty-four

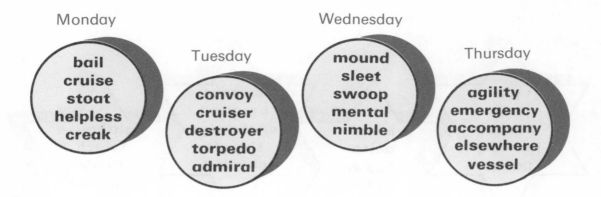

Monday

bail
cruise
stoat
helpless
creak

Tuesday

convoy
cruiser
destroyer
torpedo
admiral

Wednesday

mound
sleet
swoop
mental
nimble

Thursday

agility
emergency
accompany
elsewhere
vessel

1 *Write these sentences. Fill the spaces with words from the lists.*

a) It was decided that a cruiser should _____ the _____ of ships.

b) At the last moment, the cruiser was sent _____ because of an _____.

c) The merchant ships were _____ when a submarine launched a _____ attack upon them in the Bay of Biscay.

2 *Rearrange the letters to make the names of the shapes.*

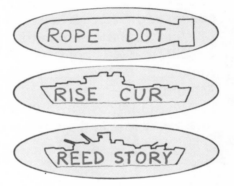

ROPE DOT

RISE CUR

REED STORY

3 *Write this limerick. Fill the spaces with words from the lists.*

A gallant old _____ named Floate
As a pet kept a fine furry _____.
On _____ and _____
It was hard not to lose her,
So she lived up the sleeve of his coat.

4 *Take letters from the end of the first word and from the beginning of the second to make list words.*
Example: **lim(b ail)ment**

harvest oats   women talk

gives seldom   denim blend

5 *Change one letter to make a list word from each of these.*

sloop   croak   ability   stout   bruise   found   fleet

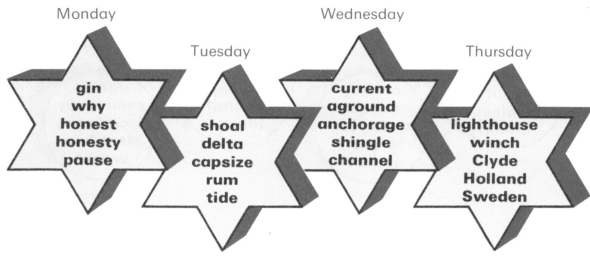

Monday
gin
why
honest
honesty
pause

Tuesday
shoal
delta
capsize
rum
tide

Wednesday
current
aground
anchorage
shingle
channel

Thursday
lighthouse
winch
Clyde
Holland
Sweden

1 *Write these sentences. Use words from the lists to fill the spaces.*
a) The _____ was built to guide ships sailing in the _____ between the Isle of Wight and the mainland.
b) Before it was built, many ships ran _____ on the _____ beaches near Milford.
c) When the _____ is full, the _____ flows very fast in the narrow channel.

2 *Use words from Monday's and Tuesday's lists to complete this puzzle.*

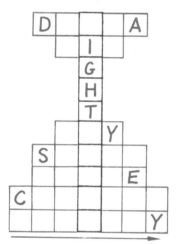

3 *Take letters from the end of the first word and from the beginning of the second to make list words.*

Example: **brigh(t ide)a**

shone steadily   model tanker
incur rental   few hyenas
twin chimpanzees   long innings
four umbrellas   dashing leader

A **delta** is a triangular - shaped area of land built up by current-borne soil at the mouth of a river. **Delta** is the Greek letter **D**, written Δ.

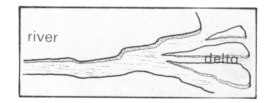

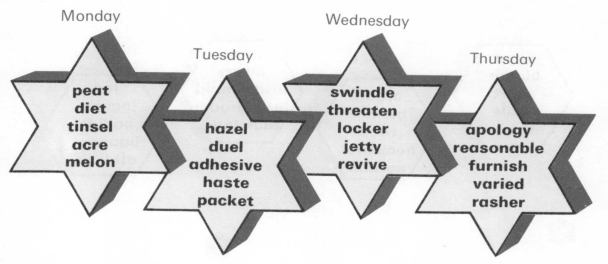

Monday: peat diet tinsel acre melon

Tuesday: hazel duel adhesive haste packet

Wednesday: swindle threaten locker jetty revive

Thursday: apology reasonable furnish varied rasher

 1 *Write these sentences. Fill the spaces with words from the lists.*

Captain Larwood demanded an _____ from Major Brooks because he thought that he was trying to _____ him at cards.

   Major Brooks started to _____ the Captain and later challenged him to a _____. The next morning, both men were in a more _____ frame of mind and they made _____ to patch up their quarrel.

 2 *Write list words which mean:*

a) glue. *b)* a slice of bacon. *c)* rotted plant life used for improving soil. *d)* a unit of land measurement. *e)* landing stage. *f)* to equip with furniture. *g)* to bring back to life.

 3 *Rearrange the letters in these words to make list words.*

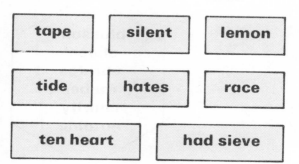

tape   silent   lemon

tide   hates   race

ten heart   had sieve

 4 *Make list words by changing the two middle letters.*

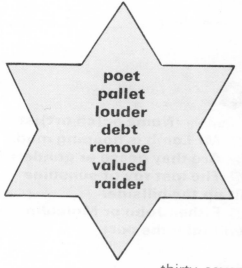

poet pallet louder debt remove valued raider

 5 *Make list words by adding two letters to:*

tins   has   lock   threat   rash   pack

thirty-seven

Monday: cape bloom chart noble stray

Tuesday: organ bishop robe beautiful normal

Wednesday: bride marry bridesmaid bridegroom marriage

Thursday: jog jogging collide bouquet athletic

1 *Write these sentences. Fill the spaces with words from the lists.*

a) Every eye was on the _____ when she came into church followed by a _____.

b) The _____ played a _____ anthem as the wedding party walked down the aisle.

c) The _____ service was conducted by the _____ of Coventry.

2 *Make list words by:*
a) changing one letter.

carry
fog
strap
formal

3 *Complete this limerick with words from Wednesday's and Thursday's lists.*

An _____ young person named West
Was _____ along full of zest
When he chanced to _____
With a newly-wed _____
Who stuffed her _____ down his vest.

b) taking away two letters.

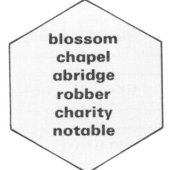

blossom
chapel
abridge
robber
charity
notable

4 *Find the list words hidden in these sentences.*
Example: **Name ea(ch art)ist**

a) **Mr Lamb is hopping mad.**

b) **Are they geese or ganders?**

c) **The last ray of sunshine lit up the hillside.**

d) **Either John or Malcolm will take the part.**

thirty-eight

Monday
bawl
chew
coral
bunk
perch

Tuesday
tidal
twilight
harpoon
yacht
wish

Wednesday
wrinkle
bracken
uneasy
gem
bristle

Thursday
appoint
appointment
headquarters
searchlight
almighty

1 *Write these sentences. Use words from the lists to fill the spaces.*

The smugglers' _____ crept into the river mouth at _____. There was a strong _____ current running and they were already late for their _____. The captain was beginning to feel _____. Suddenly, a _____ was switched on and he heard someone _____, "Surrender or we sink you."

2 *Fill in the missing letters to make list words.*

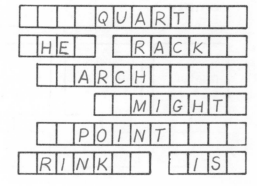

			Q	U	A	R	T		
	H	E			R	A	C	K	
		A	R	C	H				
			M		I	G	H	T	
		P	O	I	N	T			
R	I	N	K				I	S	

3 *Which of the things named in the lists might you find:*

a) on a brush? *b)* inside a parrot's cage? *c)* just below the surface of a warm sea? *d)* on a person's forehead? *e)* below decks on a ship? *f)* on the deck of a whaling ship? *g)* set in an engagement ring?

thirty-nine

JUST FOR FUN

1 Make this word chain by using the last two letters of each answer to begin the next. Example: grain > inside > devil > ill

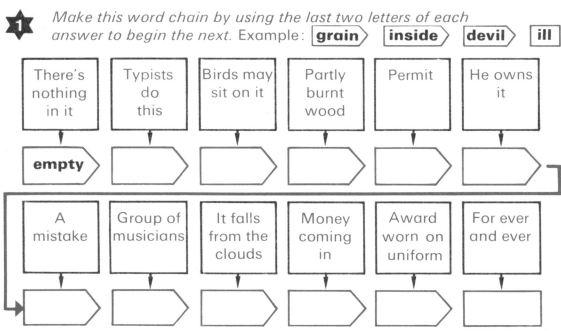

There's nothing in it	Typists do this	Birds may sit on it	Partly burnt wood	Permit	He owns it

empty >

A mistake	Group of musicians	It falls from the clouds	Money coming in	Award worn on uniform	For ever and ever

2 Write this story. Put each set of three short words together to make a longer word to fill the space occupied by the box.

The boys had sailed into the lagoon with the [ion / tent / in]

of having a [cue / be / bar]. When they heard a radio [cement / an / noun]

that the [at / her / we] was worsening, they decided to [on / band / a]

the picnic and set a [a / ring / be] for home. Soon they

encountered [mid / for / able] waves and they found the

channel through the reef [ass / able / imp]. Later a [do / a / torn] struck

the island but they made a [is / factory / sat] shelter and

huddled [her / to / get] until the storm blew itself out.

forty

3 Add a letter to the beginning and end of each of these words to make a girl's name.

all
we
an
end
ridge
rend
egg
are
tell

Monday

staff
partner
reckon
shorthand
bankrupt

Tuesday

type
typing
typist
erase
limited

Wednesday

manage
manager
salary
chairman
accountant

Thursday

employ
employer
employee
unemployed
envelope

1 *Write list words which mean:*

a) wages, usually paid monthly.   *b)* to rub out.
c) a person who looks after a company's money.
d) unable to continue in business because of
a shortage of money.   *e)* a rapid writing code.
f) the head of a board of directors.
g) a person who works for another person.
h) out of work.   *i)* to give work to.

2 *Rearrange the letters to make the names of four office jobs*

3 *Copy this frame. Write the four words from the lists which each contain four vowels into it in the correct order.*

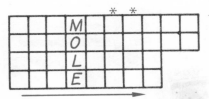

Make two non-list words from the letters in the vertical rows marked*.

4 *Take letters from the end of the first word and from the beginning of the second to make list words.*
Example: **fir(st aff)ix**

pretty petal   Roman agent
camera service
colossal Aryan
empty pistol
armchair manufacturer

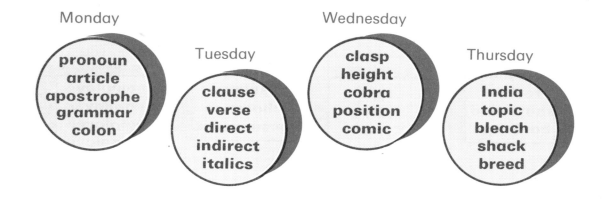

Monday — pronoun, article, apostrophe, grammar, colon

Tuesday — clause, verse, direct, indirect, italics

Wednesday — clasp, height, cobra, position, comic

Thursday — India, topic, bleach, shack, breed

1 These are examples of the use of the grammatical forms and punctuation marks named in the lists. *Complete the word or term which describes each one.*

a) "I like to skate."   d . . . . . speech

b) John's dog.   a . . . .

c) when I saw the car skid off the road   c . . . . .   *d)* **:**   c . . . .

e) Jennifer said that it was not true.   i . . . . speech

f) he   p . . . . . .

2 *Copy this frame. Use words from the lists to complete it.* The green panel will spell the name of a young animal.

C			N
C			P
C			C
C			A

3 *Take letters from the end of the first word and from the beginning of the second to make list words. Example:* **dis(co mic)rophone**

stop icing   plain diamond   fresh acknowledgement

silver service   humble achievement   sombre editor

isogram marker   calico braces

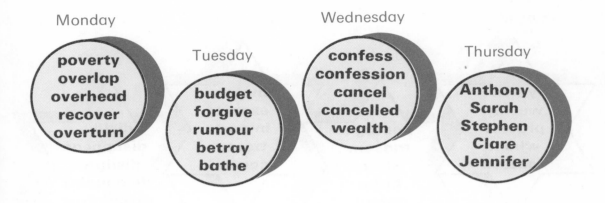

Monday
**poverty
overlap
overhead
recover
overturn**

Tuesday
**budget
forgive
rumour
betray
bathe**

Wednesday
**confess
confession
cancel
cancelled
wealth**

Thursday
**Anthony
Sarah
Stephen
Clare
Jennifer**

1 *Write these sentences. Use words from the lists to fill the spaces.*
a) When we went to _____ in the sea, we saw a sailing boat _____.
b) The spy was forced to _____ that he intended to _____ his country.
c) There is a _____ going around that the netball match has been _____.

2 *Use the letters from each pair of number plates to make names from Thursday's list.*

EA396 – CR922L
AR444S – AH9264
AYN637T – OH324N
EH956S – ETN273P

3 *Fill in the missing letters to make words from Monday's list.*

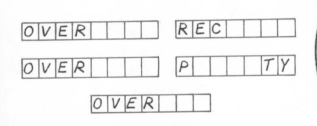

O|V|E|R| | | | R|E|C| | | |

O|V|E|R| | | | P| | | | |T|Y

O|V|E|R| | |

4 *Write list words which mean:*
a) to own up. *b)* riches.
c) state of being poor.
d) to get well. *e)* high up.
f) story which may or may not be true.

5 *Add a word from the second box to one from the first to make a list word.*

| bat   rum   step   cancel   bud
over   for   be |

| tray   give   he   led
our   get   hen   lap |

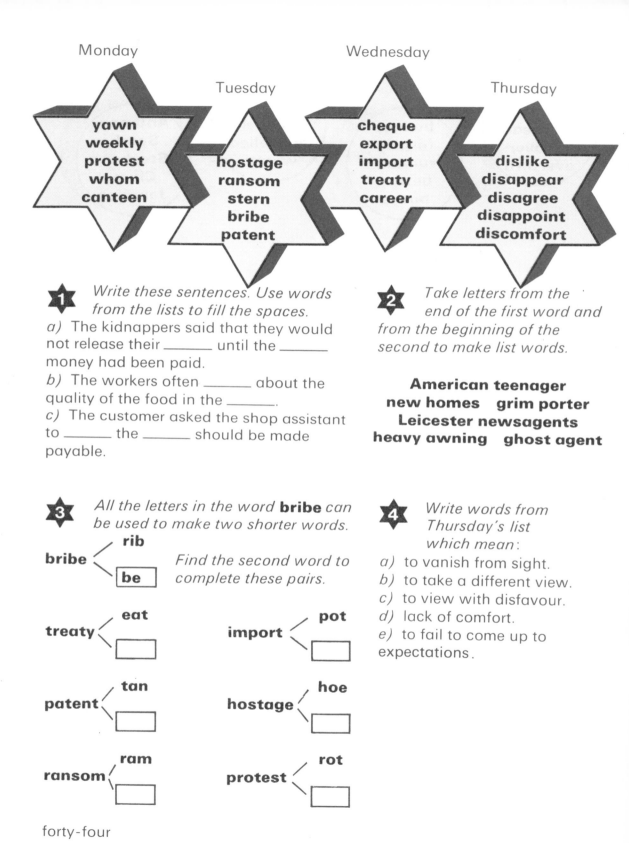

Monday

yawn
weekly
protest
whom
canteen

Tuesday

hostage
ransom
stern
bribe
patent

Wednesday

cheque
export
import
treaty
career

Thursday

dislike
disappear
disagree
disappoint
discomfort

1 Write these sentences. Use words from the lists to fill the spaces.

a) The kidnappers said that they would not release their _____ until the _____ money had been paid.

b) The workers often _____ about the quality of the food in the _____.

c) The customer asked the shop assistant to _____ the _____ should be made payable.

2 Take letters from the end of the first word and from the beginning of the second to make list words.

**American teenager
new homes   grim porter
Leicester newsagents
heavy awning   ghost agent**

3 All the letters in the word **bribe** can be used to make two shorter words.

bribe ⟨ rib / be ⟩

Find the second word to complete these pairs.

treaty ⟨ eat / ☐ ⟩   import ⟨ pot / ☐ ⟩

patent ⟨ tan / ☐ ⟩   hostage ⟨ hoe / ☐ ⟩

ransom ⟨ ram / ☐ ⟩   protest ⟨ rot / ☐ ⟩

4 Write words from Thursday's list which mean:

a) to vanish from sight.
b) to take a different view.
c) to view with disfavour.
d) lack of comfort.
e) to fail to come up to expectations.

forty-four

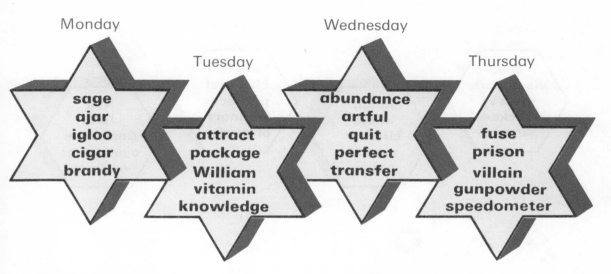

Monday: **sage ajar igloo cigar brandy**

Tuesday: **attract package William vitamin knowledge**

Wednesday: **abundance artful quit perfect transfer**

Thursday: **fuse prison villain gunpowder speedometer**

 1 *Write this limerick. Use words from Thursday's list to complete it.*

An artful young _____ named Sisson
Used some _____ to blow up a _____.
His _____ was too short
And when he was caught
Some bits of poor Sisson were missin'.

2 *Draw this frame on squared paper. Fill in the missing letters to make list words. What does the green panel spell?*

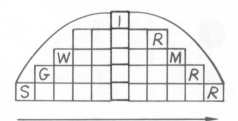

 3 *Rearrange the letters in these shapes to name the contents of each.*

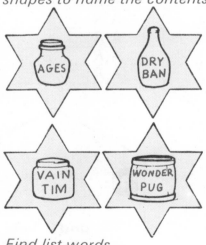

AGES

DRY BAN

VAIN TIM

WONDER PUG

 4 *Fit these parts together to make five list words.*

at	know	age	dance
a	pack	tract	bun
	ledge	jar	a

 5 *Find list words which mean:*

a) cunning, crafty. *b)* to leave behind. *c)* bad character, rogue.
d) flawless, without fault. *e)* to move from one place to another.
f) open. *g)* a plentiful supply. *h)* container or wrapping.

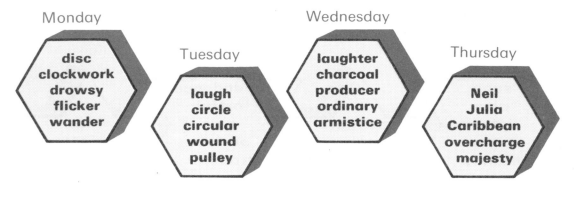

Monday
disc
clockwork
drowsy
flicker
wander

Tuesday
laugh
circle
circular
wound
pulley

Wednesday
laughter
charcoal
producer
ordinary
armistice

Thursday
Neil
Julia
Caribbean
overcharge
majesty

1 *Write these sentences. Fill the spaces with words from Monday's and Tuesday's lists.*
a) The face of the clock is a flat metal _____.
b) The clock face numbers are arranged in a _____.
c) The tip of each hand travels in a _____ path.
d) The mechanism of the clock is called _____.
e) The rope holding the weight passes round a _____.
f) The clock is _____ by pulling the weight downwards.

2 *Copy this frame. Complete it by writing in words which fit the clues.*

a) round.   b) not unusual.
c) to ask for too much payment.
d) partly burnt wood.
e) sea surrounding the West Indies.
f) declaration of peace.

					A	R		
					A	R		
					A	R		
					A	R		
					A	R		
					A	R		

3 *Rearrange these letters to make words from Wednesday's list.*

| coal arch | it is cream | earl thug |

| o i ran dry | or red cup |

4 *Find the list words which contain:*

and	lick
rib	din
jest	row
mist	arc

forty-six

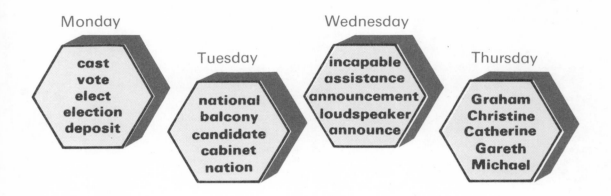

Monday

cast
vote
elect
election
deposit

Tuesday

national
balcony
candidate
cabinet
nation

Wednesday

incapable
assistance
announcement
loudspeaker
announce

Thursday

Graham
Christine
Catherine
Gareth
Michael

1 Write these sentences. Use words from the lists to fill the spaces.

a) The _____ of the result of the _____ will be made at midnight.

b) The Mayor will _____ the total number of votes _____ and the name of the winner from the town hall _____.

c) The _____ with the largest total _____ will be the new Member of Parliament.

2 Change the first two letters in each of these to make a list word.

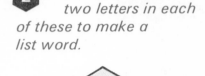

denounce
optional
late   post
lotion
resistance

3 Arrange the three small words in each box into a list word which fits the meaning.

a) help given to a person who needs it | I stance ass |

b) a statement made to the public | an cement noun |

c) lacking the power to do something | able in cap |

d) a person who hopes to be elected | did ate can |

e) a committee of government ministers | net I cab |

4 Rearrange the letters to make list names.
their cane
lace him
chins tire

5 Who is the successful **candidate**?

Candidate	votes cast
Catherine Beal	5 378
Graham Parker	2 049
Gareth Edwards	9 287

Index to words in Book 5